POEMS OF MY HOMELAND

IRISH POEMS FROM THE
HEART

Poems of my Homeland

Irish Poems from the Heart

by

DG Tandra

Pesky Publishing Ltd

Copyright © 2025 DG Tandra and Pesky Publishing Ltd

All rights reserved. No part of this publication may be reproduced, stored or transmitted in any form or by any means, electronic, mechanical, photocopying, recording, scanning, or otherwise without written permission from the publisher. It is illegal to copy this book, post it to a website, or distribute it by any other means without permission.

Cover design and front cover image copyright of Curtis Gordon, 3D Artist/Illustrator.

Pesky Publishing™ is a registered trademark of Pesky Publishing Ltd

First edition: 2025

ISBN 978-1-7396901-5-1

Published by Pesky Publishing Ltd

Acknowledgements

A word of sincere thanks to Mr Patrick Dobson and to my wife Allison. They both helped make this publication possible, by ironing out the 'creases' and, where necessary, making grammatical corrections. Indeed, without that support and encouragement from my wife Allison, this book may never have seen the light of day.

Contents

Acknowledgements — iii

About The Author — 1

What is a Poem? — 2

The True Voice of Ireland! — 3

An Irish Invitation! — 6

The Luck of the Irish! — 9

The Tales of an Irish Peregrinator! — 12

Reminiscing those good old days — 14

My Old Irish Homestead! — 16

Shattered dreams! — 19

My Irish Homeland! — 22

My Old Irish Wishing Well! — 27

Yer Man's Special Day! — 29

Can't Stop Remembering My Irish Rose Forever!	30
My Irish Rose	32
I'm Wishing!	34
Freedom's Just Trail!	36
No going back to the past	38
Erin Go Bragh!	40
An Irish Star! (Tribute to Seamus Heaney)	43
Rainbow over Ireland!	45
Christmas Eve Night!	46
Belfast is Buzzing again!	49
A Dream for Peace!	51
Erin's best	53
Peace at Last!	54

About The Author

This selection of poems is the work of D. G. Tandra. David is now retired, but as a husband, dad, grandfather and great grandfather, he took time away from his busy life to write poems and short stories for the enjoyment of family and friends. This particular selection of poems is very dear to his heart. Born in Tandragee in that one fair county in Ireland - Armagh, known as the Orchard County because of the wealth of apple orchards, where memories so glorious and grand were made and love for the land of his birth compelled him to put pen to paper and share his love in this short selection from his heart. David would be delighted if this wee taste of home whet the appetite of the reader to visit the Emerald Isle and see for themselves the wonder of it all !!

What is a Poem?

A poem is a succinct story,
That's worth every telling it gets,
The feelings of the poet's heart,
Expressed in verity or myth,
The recollection of memories,
Whatever they might be,
The hopes and dreams of every good,
Brought to reality!

The True Voice of Ireland!

I am the true voice of Ireland, calling loud and clear,
I speak with supreme authority so let everyone give ear!
What I've to say's important, it is coming from my heart,
So, I ask that you will listen, and also play your part!

Too long I reigned in silence, a mute upon my throne,
Now I must break the silence, speak for myself alone!
Many voices have been raised; all claim to speak for me,
I authorized not one of them they assumed such liberty!

Many adjectives they did employ, some have honoured me,
Alas, others caused a broken heart, by misrepresenting me,
Some talk in their pomposity of setting Ireland free,
I'll have them know I'm no prisoner I have my autonomy!

I've looked in anger and disgust at the carnage and the pain,
Some so-called "Sons of Ireland" have inflicted once again,
Innocent blood stains my streets, and my forty shades of green,
Another dark day for me to mourn, what I have heard and seen!

Not in my name did you do those deeds, don't dare say in Ireland's cause,
My cause is not murder and mayhem, but that, which it always was,
Love, peace, respect, toleration, help, and care for everyone,
You, the very antithesis, hatred, bitterness, terrorism, the gun!

Don't make any boast of loving me, the Emerald Isle of the sea,
Your boastful words are vacuous, as your actions with your words don't agree,
Illegal guns in possession, and hatred within your heart,
Components for disaster, with such I won't be a part.

I am the true voice of Ireland, North, South, East and West,
Speaking on my own behalf, and for millions who want the best,
For me and all my people, whatever persuasion they may be,
I'm working for a better day, for real lasting tranquillity!

I am the true voice of Ireland, and with me my people agree,
We don't need your bombs or bullets, to keep us company,
Your instruments of destruction need decommissioned from the fight,

Poems of my Homeland

Then in every corner of my land the future will be bright!

There is a future bright for all, who want their future bright,
The way to it won't be easy, as we struggle with wrongs and with right,
But to know the last bomb has exploded, the last bullet fired from the gun,
Will be well worth all the struggles we made, and all the hard work that was done!

I am the true voice of Ireland, calling loud and clear,
I speak with supreme authority so let everyone give ear,
I'm going forward not backward, away from the ghosts of the past,
There's a new dawn that has broken over Ireland, there is hope in my land at last!

An Irish Invitation!

Come accept the invitation to visit the Emerald Isle,
The land of Saints and Scholars, and sojourn a little while,
Make full the life you're living, deprive yourself of naught,
Surround yourself with Ireland's best, why should you suffer loss.

Come enjoy her welcomes, there's a hundred thousand and more,
Enjoy her lively music that causes foot tapping on the floor,
Join in the singing of the songs, with great gusto raise the roof,
There's happiness in Ireland, such singing is the proof.

Come enjoy the Irish humour, the craic and stories that are told,
Visit the many enchanting Glens that will seize upon your soul,
Tread quietly and silently, softer, than a whisper goes,
Look for tiny creatures; watch how your excitement will grow,

The surprise of your life awaits you, when Ireland's little creatures appear,
They skip, they dance, they sing their songs, sweet music to the ear,

Poems of my Homeland

They are gifted entertainers dedicated to the "Glens Show,'"
Wherever you go in Ireland they will set your face a glow.

Come be part of life in Ireland, even for a little while,
A visit to the old country produces miles of smile,
Tread the land our forefathers trod, with pride within the breast,
It had its fears, fights, and famine, yet it triumphed in every test,

Come trace your roots in Ireland, that's where they are found,
Cause the past to live again, as you walk on sacred ground,
Stand still awhile and listen well, hear voices from the past,
Our ancestors calling out to us, shouting, Ireland first not last!

Come experience the wonders of her intoxicating charm,
Soak up the Irish magic as it wraps you like an arm,
View the forty shades of green and kiss the Blarney Stone,
Make a wish at the wishing well; keep it secret until it is known.

Come accept the invitation to visit our enchanted Isle,
Listen to the tales that's told, they're sure to bring a smile,

There is no exaggeration; they all are gospel truth,
The teller of the stories always has a lasting drooth.

Come and visit Ireland, disappointed you will not be,
Play your part for that special place, the Emerald Isle of the sea,
Come raise your voice for Ireland and tell to one and all,
I accepted her invitation; I answered Ireland's call!

The Luck of the Irish!

She wished me the luck of the Irish, as I strolled slowly by,
A beautiful smile was on her face, a teasing glint in her eye,
Her pearly white teeth and her long curly hair, a beauty none can deny,
A sweet Irish Colleen, the girl of any man's dream and that my friend is no lie!

And what is the luck of the Irish I asked? as I applied the brakes to my stroll,
Didn't want to go any farther, this beauty had captured my soul,
A tingling sensation danced on my spine, like fairies engaged in full play,
If there's such a thing as the luck of the Irish, it was on my side, that day!

The more that I viewed her the more I desired her, this Colleen sent down from above,
Her prisoner forever I'd happily be, locked into her prison of love!
No prison chores too arduous, nor a lifetime sentence too long,
With her as my warden no complaint would I make, she'd be the theme of my song!

"And what is the luck of the Irish?" I repeated the question again,
"Tell me all there is to know, so take the time and explain,
Commence at the very beginning, tiptoe right through to the end,
As I'm not the brightest bulb in the lamp, move slowly as you explain."

She smiled a broad smile at what I had said, so broad it kissed each of her ears,
"The luck of the Irish, I'd have you to know, will strip from you worries and fears,
Its goodness not badness, light and not darkness, blessings, and lots of good cheer,
With the luck of the Irish, good fortune is with you, making your pathway clear!"

"It never will hurt, harm or harass you, its aim is to sweeten life's way,
It knows nothing of bitterness or hatred, but exists to brighten your day,
It is so, so very special, more valuable than silver or gold,
Its best to have the luck of the Irish, since it can't be bought nor sold!

So have it with you wherever you go, you got it when I wished it to you,
It's always on the side of right, so be right in all that that you do,
Use it well and use it wisely, see all you dreams come true,

If you treat it right and give it its place, you'll succeed in
all that you do."

I thanked sincerely that sweet Irish Colleen, for making
the wish for me,
The luck of the Irish does it really work? I thought, I'll
test it and see,
So I quickly reciprocated, whereupon she raced at me,
Throwing our arms around each other, we were locked
in harmony.

I wish you the luck of the Irish, whoever and wherever
you are,
You might be at home here in Ireland; it could be that
you are afar,
Don't imagine that your location has ruled you out of
bounds,
I assure you the luck of the Irish, can reach you
wherever you're found!

She wished me the luck of the Irish, how lucky I came
to be,
That day I met the love of my life and the creme de la
creme for me,
All because a sweet Irish Colleen, with a teasing glint in
her eye,
Wished me the luck of the Irish, as I strolled slowly by!

The Tales of an Irish Peregrinator!

I've been over this country from the North to the South,
And there isn't a town that I haven't tried out,
There isn't a highway a road or a lane,
That I haven't travelled in sunshine or rain.

I've gone to the East, and I've gone to the West,
And it's hard to say what part is the best,
I went where the Mournes sweep down to the sea,
Then across country to lovely Tralee!

I went to Killarney and then Skibbereen,
I then travelled North by the coast road it seemed,
For I passed through the towns of Wicklow and Bray,
And it took me some time—ah the best part of a day.

I went to Ahoghill just East of the Bann,
T'was there that I met with a fool of a man,
For his hens were laying their eggs all about,
And the silly fool thought their inside had dropped out.

I saw some strange things as I travelled around,
I remember one night as I camped out of town,
Sure there to my right deep down was a glen,
I declare it was filled with little green men!

One night as I entered a town in the West,
I saw forty pigs each dressed in a vest,
When I asked for the reason, I politely was told,

Poems of my Homeland

That the vest was the secret of good pork being sold!

And then I must tell you about the red hen,
That could draw like an artist, used its beak as a pen,
It was truly amazing for it could swim on its back,
And the eggs that it laid were all coloured black!

And then there's the donkey that wouldn't go BRAY!
But protested because of the cut in its hay,
It was the watch guard who silent did keep,
Until its own master its demands did meet!

Then I climbed on the rainbow for sure I was told,
That right at its end was a big pot of gold,
And sure, there enough as the pot I did spy,
The rainbow it vanished, and I fell from the sky.

So, you see I have travelled North, South, East and West,
I have stories to tell, but like all the rest,
Somethings you may question and ask are they true?
Well, the believing of them, I'll leave that with you!

Reminiscing those good old days

I took a stroll down memory lane as I returned back home,
For I had been away for years to see the world, did roam,
I stood on every Continent and sailed the seven seas,
I saw the wonders of the world but none of them did please,
Half as much as what I saw in this my native land,
It makes me proud that I can boast, "I am an Irish man."

As the pages of my memory turn-over one by one,
I recall those youthful days of excitement, laughter, fun,
When Mum and Dad and siblings all our country did explore,
From East to West then from the South to our farthest Northern shore,
Oh, I remember well those days and the sights that I did see,
When I was just a little lad living life worry free.

I saw the Giant's Causeway a wonder to behold,
Then I walked the walls of Derry and heard strange stories told,
From Derry's walls to City halls, to Castles by the sea,
Then to the Glens of Antrim for peace and tranquility!
Oh, I remember well those days when I was just a lad,
As I travelled o'er our country with my siblings, my

Poems of my Homeland

Mum and Dad.

There are many other beauty spots as a family we did see,
Like the Majestic Mourne Mountains that go sweeping to the sea,
The Silent Valley, the Spelga Dam, and the Blue Lake Mountain high,
And Slieve Donard, giant of the Mournes stretching to the sky!
Oh, I remember well those days as a happy family!
We travelled North, South, East and West to see what we could see!

I'm thankful for the memories of those days long ago,
For the excitement and adventure as a family we did know,
Five decades and a little more have quickly passed away,
My youth has gone, I now am old my hair is silver gray,
I saw the wonders of the world as through it I did roam,
But I'd have you know in all the world, there is no place like Home!

My Old Irish Homestead!

It was good to be home again, my first in forty years,
As I viewed the old homestead I, broke down in tears,
The sight that met me caused great shock, and pained me at my heart,
The place that bore witness to my birth was, literally falling apart!

This old homestead of ours no longer looked the same,
As it did when I left it, my fortune to obtain,
The windows all were shattered the doors were missing too!
The well-thatched roof that Dad did keep had all but fallen through!

As I stood transfixed and saddened the sight that I did see,
I could not believe that such a sight was staring back at me,
That old homestead I had loved so well, with sorrow I must tell,
Had bowed to the inevitable, and to the world bids its own farewell!

Its former glory had departed it now is a broken shell,
A picture full of weariness and loneliness as well,
It once was so inviting with a warm welcome to one and all,
Who took the time to visit who took the time to call!

I remember well those happy times for they all excited me,
When neighbours came to ceilidh what craic there used to be!
We had homemade entertainment with stories, jokes, and song,
Finished off with Mum's apple tart, and tea that was donkey strong.

I love this my old homestead though it's seen a better day,
A million precious memories in my mind have come to play,
I hear the sweetness of Mum's voice, and hear Dad's earnest prayer,
As he asks that God Almighty will, keep me in His loving care!

I love this my old homestead though now the worst for wear!
When Dad and Mum were building it, they placed each stone with prayer,
They taught profitable lessons as they sought to raise me right,
In this our old homestead for me they were, a guiding light!

'Twas here I first heard my parents voice 'twas here I learnt my name,
'Twas here I learnt to crawl, to walk and play my childish game,

'Twas here I was taught right from wrong, and must never be to blame,
For any wrong to man or beast but be guiltless of such shame!

Our old homestead was a sanctuary where we had peace and rest,
All who entered through its door, were well and truly blest,
No one was ever turned away who sought its warm embrace,
All who came were warmly welcomed irrespective, of colour, creed, or race!

The old homestead now is silent; the jokes and laughter gone,
There is now no home entertainment, no singing our old favourite song,
No gathering of folks for a ceilidh no new stories to gossip around,
No foot tapping on the hard tiled floor to the fiddler's tuneful sound!

A beautiful era has ended; Mum and Dad have now left this shore,
They have gone to a heavenly homestead and don't need the old one anymore,
In their last letter to me they promised, to meet me at heaven's open door,
Then they'll show me around our new homestead where, we'll abide forever more!

Shattered dreams!

I sailed away from Ireland, thinking t'was the right thing to do,
The days were dark, times were hard, I saw no other way through,
I had heard so many stories of new life beyond our shore,
Promises of wealth and plenty, I ventured to explore.

I sailed away from Ireland, with dreams and plans galore,
I said goodbye to hardships, my struggling days were o'er,
I sailed the wild Atlantic, deep, dangerous, and blue,
In search of that better life where every dream comes true!

As I sailed away from Ireland, joy bells in my heart did ring,
A new world lay before me; such caused me a song to sing,
I'll make it in this new world BIG, the BIGGEST there can be!
I'll climb the ladder of success, there'll be no stopping me!

I'll be diligent and indefatigable; praise and glory shall come my way,

I'll be part of high society; with the elite I'll live and play!
I'm neither supercilious nor egotistical but this I'll say,
In anybody's company, I'm the one that makes the day!

I sailed away from Ireland, with my head stuck in the air,
I never had a worry; I never had a care,
There was no negativity within this heart of mine,
Positivity reigned supreme, it for me did shine!

I made it to the "Promised Land" with much get up and go,
But dreams are not reality, soon this I came to know,
The dreams I had all vanished like the phantom will-o-the-wisp,
Alas there was more substance in the winter evening mist.

Initially everything was great, there were those who gave much and more,
The dreams I had then faded when, reality banged on my door,
Keep your nose clean and do what you're told or for you there'll be no more,
I realized it there and then that the honeymoon period was o'er.

I sailed away from Ireland, thinking t'was the right thing to do,
But I have learnt the hard way; our thoughts are not always true,

Poems of my Homeland

Those far off fields seem lush and green, deceiving to the eye,
But the fields at home out green them all, that no one can deny!

I now am back home in Ireland, and happy so to be,
Those happenings that happened, far across the sea,
Brought reality home to me and opened my eyes to see,
If I were to retain my sanity then, those foreign lands I must flee!

Flee them I did empty handed, I was glad to get away,
Nothing of value did I bring home, Shattered Dreams produces no pay,
I bid adieu to tyrannical ways, goodbye to their whole wicked schemes,
I came back home for I will not live a life of Shattered Dreams.

My Irish Homeland!

They asked me about my homeland as they bragged about their own,
Some said they have Canyons great, unique to them alone,
Others exulted in their waterfalls tumbling, o'er the precipice,
While the Great Wall of China for others topped their list!

I told them we had no canyons that, with theirs would compare,
No great waterfalls or lengthy wall for such are very rare,
No Taj Mahal, no Eiffel Tower, no Statue of Liberty,
What we have is a beautiful land where its people are happy and free!

My Homeland is an Island where Saint Patrick's Shamrock grows,
When God made it, He planted seeds to germinate and grow,
And so, on 17th Day of March, wherever you may go,
A sprig of Saint Patrick Shamrock is a help to make you glow.

Intrinsic to my homeland are the mountains and the moors,
The lowlands and the lake lands with terrestrial contours,

Poems of my Homeland

The famous Slemish Mountain, Saint Patrick's first known Irish home,
T'was there as shepherd of the sheep our patron Saint did roam!

The city walls of Derry or Londonderry if you please,
The lush green Glens of Antrim where you'll find rest and ease,
The famous Giants Causeway and I'm proud to make this boast,
All these are part of my homeland, and I don't mean to gloat.

The Atlantic Drive on my homeland Isle with its undulating way,
Has captivating beauty that would take one's breath away,
From Slieve League cliffs in Donegal to Cork's famous Bantry Bay,
This Atlantic Drive with unrivalled vistas, in your memory forever will stay.

My homeland's a cornucopia, it has an inexhaustible store,
From North to South, East to West from inland to the seashore,
It has something to tickle each fancy, causing a craving for more,
Whatever it is that you fancy will be found in my homeland's full store.

Sport, history, music, dancing, singing, great craic and folklore,
Stories of strange little creatures, that if seen bring good luck to your door,
Also, every year to my homeland, thousands travel for to see,
The beauty of County Kerry, but more especially the Rose of Tralee!

My homeland shares its beauty and bounty with all and everyone,
Its entertainments and amusements are a recipe for fun,
One kiss on the Blarney Stone and you'll be feeling really fab,
But be warned for that one kiss endows with the gift of the gab!

I've a duty to warn every husband to stay clear of the famed Blarney Stone,
If a wife ever gets to kiss it, with much talk at her mouth she will foam,
Take her to the lakes of Fermanagh, Killarney, or Portballintrae,
Be warned if she kisses the Blarney her tongue will not last her day.

In every part of my homeland North, South, East and West,
There's a hundred thousand welcomes which buoys the soul with zest,
Producing invigoration, motivation, expectation, and participation,

With these the only outcome is, a marvellous celebration.

The land of Saints and Scholars that's the place that is my home,
Many I know have left it, in foreign lands to roam,
Their adopted lands have their support and they're glad to be a part,
But their first love is my homeland 'tis always in their heart.

They miss its warmest wishes, its wonders and its woo,
No matter where on earth they go to it they will be true,
And when a chance comes their way, a home visit for to pay,
They will grasp the opportunity and gladly seize the day.

Visitors to my homeland are smitten by it from the start,
It's charm, craic and cheerfulness go straight to their heart,
Our different traditions and culture, should not bring division or strife,
For diversity is variety and variety, the spice of life!

There is plenty of spice in my homeland, we have enough and to spare,
I invite you to come pay us a visit, I promise for you there's a share,
And as you inhale air ethereal, and spellbound by the sights that you see,

Like one of old I know you will say, "the half was never told me."

Fair homeland of God's creation, creme de la creme you are to me,
Land of my birth and upbringing, may I always be true to thee,
Land of my father and forefathers' now the land of me,
With extended arm I salute you, oh island of the sea.

My Old Irish Wishing Well!

I sat for a while on the Old Wishing Well,
As I did in my childhood, when to it I did tell,
My wishes my worries my dreams and my fears,
Now I'm reminiscing of those far away years.

I recall indubitably the fun that we had,
With my siblings and friends when I was a lad,
I remember the wishes I made way back then,
For I secretly made them again and again!

As I sat for a while on the Old Wishing Well,
I thought of the stories I know it could tell,
It heard many secrets yet, concealed everyone,
I knew I could trust it, not to tell anyone!

At the Old Wishing Well we created much fun,
As children we played games, as children we sung,
Songs to the wishing well, to keep it on side,
That all of our wishes would be realised!

At the Old Wishing Well there first I did see,
A beauty so tender none fairer than she,
Her eyes were like diamonds her teeth like pure pearl,
The wish that I made then was, 'that she'd be my girl.'

The Old Wishing Well had been so good to me,
It granted my wish, and that girl come to be,
My childhood sweetheart, then in later years,
Took my name as hers, midst good wishes and cheers.

We wed in the Church where we both said, "I will."
Then to the Old Wishing Well just to add to the thrill,
And wow! What a sight there was on display,
The Old Wishing Well was a cornucopia that day!

As I sat there musing and recalling the past,
I relived many moments that never died but did last,
I could hear voices calling to me across time,
Among them the sweet voice of my own Valentine!

We had a great life together, this Old Wishing Well team,
We worked hand in glove to fulfil each other's dream,
Then suddenly she was taken to God's home in the sky,
I have pondered and questioned to understand why!

She knew she was leaving me, told me not to cry,
"Promise you'll do this for me, when I take to the sky,
Go, to the Old Wishing Well where we fell in love,
Make a wish that us both, will meet in heaven above."

So that's why I'm here at the Old Wishing Well,
My promise I'm keeping as the Angels can tell,
I've asked that God also will keep us safe in His love,
'Till we are reunited, in His home up above!

Yer Man's Special Day!

It is his day a special day that belongs to him alone,
yet millions gather in his name, his honour to make known,
On his day the world awakes, a participant wants to be,
part of the laughter and the fun and what makes jubilee.

There is singing there is dancing there are marching bands and more.
There is skipping and applauding and much cheering to the fore,
There are shouts of wild excitement thunderous is the roar,
When he whose appointed day had come 'yer man' the one we all adore.

He is known the whole world over, from every corner they do come,
Bringing with them greetings now a new term had begun.
Good wishes are exchanged by all, not one word went astray,
From the rising of the sun, until the dying of the day,

Whose is this day, this special day? why he's 'yer man' of worldwide fame,
Man of faith and friendship _____ is his name. * See Page 57

Can't Stop Remembering My Irish Rose Forever!

l can't stop remembering no matter how I try,
The love we shared together won't let me say goodbye,
I sec you every minute of every waking day,
Every night you're in my dreams, you just won't go away.

I hear the sweetness in your voice; see the twinkle in your eye,
The love of my life you'll always be, that's truth and is no lie!
Your captivating smiles l see, still feel your gentle touch,
Living life without you, has robbed us of so much!

Living life is not easy now that you've gone away,
You're etched on my memory; you're in my heart to stay!
My love for you my darling, grows stronger day by day,
I'll only stop remembering when the sun has no golden ray!

I can't stop remembering, no matter how I try,
The good times we had together don't wither away and die,
They're alive within my memory, I hope in yours as well,
I'd give the world if I had it to give, just to have you as my belle!

Poems of my Homeland

I can't stop remembering, believe me how I try,
The love we had together won't let me say goodbye.
Without you, life is empty, no melodious lullaby.
I cannot stop remembering, I will love you 'till I die!

You are my Irish rose forever; I'll never say goodbye!

My Irish Rose

There is a flower in Country Donegal,
To me the fairest flower of all,
In Irish soil this flower does grow,
It is my rose from sweet Raphoe.

My Irish Rose, sweet Irish Rose,
To me the fairest flower that grows,
The yellow Rose of Texas rare,
To you my love could not compare.

I loved you when I first did see,
Your beauty when you smiled at me,
My heart was captured by the sight,
I had of you on that first night,

Then one day in the country,
We carved our names on a big oak tree,
A little heart and an arrow too,
A symbol that our love was true.

T'was then we planned how things should be.
I with you, and you with me
My heart that day filled with delight,
When you said that you would be my wife.

You are all I ever hoped for, but there is much, so much more,
there is life, love, and laughter all this in a full store.

Poems of my Homeland

You're a petal that never withers, never falls unto the ground,
And compared to other roses you're the best that can be found.

My Irish Rose

I'm Wishing!

For an Irish Traditional Way

I wish the powers were granted me, to bring back the days that are gone,
to put a stop to the rolling days that, hasten old age along,
to relive again those far away days, to embrace them, their laughter, their fun,
to have our yesterdays today, would be welcomed by many a one.

Those good old days of long ago, hold memories precious and dear,
when family and friends gathered in our house, for a bit of craic and cheer,
sadly, things are much different now, there is silence in the house of my birth,
for Mum and Dad, siblings, and friends, have all gone the way of the earth!

How I wish the powers were granted me, to call back the years that are gone,
those youthful, carefree, happy days, would be present and singing a song,
there would be a great reunion, and we'd ceilidh the night away,
drunken with the many tales and yarns, told, in the Irish traditional way!

Poems of my Homeland

There's is no crime in wishing, for such lightens life's highway,
such can cause a light to shine, to brighten a dark lonely day,
one good thing about wishing, it can be done wherever you are,
you can wish on whatever you want to, not essential to wish on a star!

I won't ever give up wishing, for it never has given up me,
as long as I live, I'll have it, keeping me company!

Freedom's Just Trail!

Come walk with us, as we march along,
On freedom's just trail righting the wrong,
Making the world a much better place,
For all peoples irrespective of colour, or race.

As we in this mission that just onward go,
United in purpose against a real foe,
Of racism, poverty, war, and greed,
Our aspiration, to save a world in need!

As each of us do what little we can,
Our little together can accomplish our plan,
For my little and your little will rise mountain high,
As onward we go our foe to decry!

So, as we march onward on freedom's just trail,
A most difficult road yet, right will prevail,
Whatever confronts us we'll take in our stride,
Neither threatenings nor menacing shall turn us aside!

The hills they are high and the valleys so deep,
Yet we'll keep on going, our promise to keep,
To help make this world a much better place,
Free from that cruel, callous monster of hate.

Eradication, is the name for this game,
Rooting out racism and whatever's the same,
This cause is principled, honourable, and just,

Poems of my Homeland

With determination and respect, we will do what we must!

Let's not waste our life, for we only get the one,
Let's make an impression, let good work be done,
Let's not live to be useless for sadly some do,
Let's live to be missed when our life is through!

So come walk with us on freedom's just trail,
Be part of the movement that against wrong shall prevail,
Oppose this our foe; stand up for the right,
Till we see our world rid, of this awful plight!

This foe is the trouble wherever it goes,
Its baggage is heartache, tears, sorrows and woes,
The world would be a much better place,
If this troubler was removed from the whole human race!

Let the foe die the death, and bury it deep,
Let none mourn its passing, let none for it weep,
It pained many millions, caused its millions to die,
So good riddance to racism and its cohorts, goodbye!

Let no eulogies be given at it passing away,
Its demise will usher in a bright blue-sky day,
Mission then accomplished, the righteous cause did not fail,
All because of the impact of freedom's just trail.

No going back to the past
Onward together we brighten our tomorrows!

Going back to the past our today shouts, NO, NO, NO!
We've had enough of the killings, enough of the woe,
Enough of the heartache the tears and the pain,
Our yesterday's dark past must never happen again.

We are the masters of tomorrow; the future is in our hands,
The causes of our troubled past must have no support to stand,
The bitterness, the hatred the stubbornness and more,
Must be buried in the deepest grave with goodbye forever more.

Excuses must not be allowed to drag our dark past along,
To live in the darkness of the past, prompts dangers that are wrong,
Strive for a future bright, its fruit of laughter and fun,
Life lived without the wickedness, bigotry, or the gun.

Tomorrow's days arc in our hands, so handle carefully,
Let's plan for life and all its joys, not death or misery,
Retrograde steps we must not take, but forward we must go,
To build a better future where love and peace will grow.

Poems of my Homeland

Let the dark past be where it is, resurrected it must not be,
There must be no going back to those days of misery,
A healing balm has been applied for a diagnosis found,
So onward, forward, and upward, we are now on solid ground.

People of Ireland seize the day and wear the victor's Crown!

Erin Go Bragh!

Ireland, Hibernia, Erin, Airlann, Emerald of the Sea,
Not another country in the world means as much to me,
Land of my birth and breeding, land of my life and love,
Your beauty enchants and thrills me; you're a gift from God above!

Land of Saints and Scholars, of sport and songs galore,
And the tap, tap, tap of the Irish dance causes encore uproar,
Land of mythology and folklore at times difficult to comprehend,
Yet, an audience with the little green men brings the enigma to an end!

Land that embraces 4 Provinces, Ulster, Munster, Leinster, and Connaught, with 32 Counties in all,
Travel where you will North, South, East or West a hundred thousand welcomes will call,
And you're sure to meet Politicians, Poachers, Protesters, Poets, Preachers, and Psychics and many more besides,
All pontificating their panacea, in cities or by the country roadside!

Land of life and laughter, music and the dance, land of magnetism attracting true romance,

Poems of my Homeland

Where boy meets girl, and girl meets boy was their meeting all by chance?
It was part of the magic of the Emerald Isle, that they found their true romance!
So, three cheers for the island of Ireland for it only took the one glance!

Land of lakes and mountains and rivers running deep,
land of air ethereal inducing perfect sleep,
'Tis my home sweet home where I toil and reap,
where I laugh and sing where I cry and weep,

To it I speak my troubles my worries and my fears,
my joys, and expectations my plans for future years,
Ireland, Hibernia, Erin, Airlann my land so dear,
never once refused to hear!

My allegiance is to this dear land and because of this I will,
Do all the good I can to promote her health, not ill!
Nought of hurt will she cause to anyone, to you she'll do no wrong,
But she'll do her best to thrill your soul as you listen to her song.

This is a homely land, its welcomes outshine the sun,
Come in peace and you're welcome there's an invite to join in the fun!
Take a seat at the open fire with a mug of tea and a bun,
Then enjoy from the griddle a hot soda farl lured by butter on the run.

Land of the blarney stone, and the remains of King Brian Boru,
Saint Patrick made his home in her to his calling he ever was true,
From Slemish in County Antrim across the land he did go,
Bringing the good news of salvation for everyone to know

Land famed throughout the world for her forty shades of green,
People stroll them; singers' sing them; some even lie down to dream,
Another special that's unique to her, is the soul thrilling River Dance,
Whose steps in the programme tapped out on the stage have a message of peace, love, and romance!

Land that had known its troubles, thank God they are all in the past,
The dark threatening clouds that blanketed the sun were not allowed to last,
The men of the night her destruction they sought, but their objective they failed to obtain,
And because of that I say Erin go bragh not once, but again and again!

Erin go bragh, Erin go bragh you're the love of millions worldwide,
Erin go bragh, Erin go bragh such love we never will hide!

An Irish Star! (Tribute to Seamus Heaney)

He was born as a baby just like the rest of us,
He was indeed a goodly child, his parents delight, and fuss!
He was the Son of pure Irish soil, and proud that it was so,
Born and bred in Ireland, proud to have the whole world know!

He was a boy from the country, who never forgot his roots,
Never forgot the wee bowl he was baked in, his life produced much fruit,
A husband and a family man, a true friend through and through,
A gentleman, a scholar, and a willing helper too!

A man of many talents, with achievements to match each one,
Professor of Poetry at Oxford, Nobel prize in literature he won,
Some ascribe to him the appellation of being Ireland's Poet, Number One,
Ireland is proud to own him, her truly prolific Son.

He climbed the ladder of success, his talents caused it so,
From obscurity to worldwide fame, Seamus Heaney now they know,
He was a Star an Irish Star, shining bright in the ebony night,

Making life a much better place, with his words not of wrong but right.

This Master of the written word has retired from this scene of time,
Yet we hear him speaking to us, in every verse and every line,
The legacy that he left us will never fade nor die,
The poetry of Seamus Heaney doesn't use the word goodbye.

The work he did is enduring it will never wither and die,
He, the genius behind it all, was always reaching for the sky,
Though now gone from us not forgotten, respected by those near and far,
He touched the lives of millions, Ireland's Own Bright Shining Star!

This Star will never tarnish; such will not be his foe,
The beauty of his sparkle will cause the world to know,
That, the baby became an adult, the adult became a star.
Who shines like the sun in the heavens, outshining all others by far!

Rainbow over Ireland!

Oh, rainbow in the sky so high,
I wish that you would grant that I,
Could have your colours for a while,
To bring your beauty into style!

You spread your lovely colours bright,
Above the earth, such a delight,
Red, Orange, Green and Indigo
With Yellow, Blue and Violet glow.

Your beauty bids us lift our eyes,
And view you arched high in the skies,
It matters not sunshine or rain,
Your beauty always remains the same.

And when the storm has gathered near,
And the thunder roar is all we hear,
The dark clouds lose their threatening hue,
As soon as you appear to view!

So, rainbow with your colours bright,
With beauty that's such a wonderous sight,
God's promise you eloquently proclaim,
A universal flood there'll never be again!

Christmas Eve Night!

The night before Christmas was cold but bright,
For the moon in full strength cast its silvery light,
While the heavenly stars scintillating above,
Reminded me that Christmas is the season of love!

As I stood in the cold that winter's night,
Looking up to the heavens, I saw Santa in flight,
His Reindeer in unison striking the air,
As they sped on their journey to "Everywhere."

The sleigh was stacked high with presents galore,
He would distribute each load and fly home for more,
For the children all over the world fell asleep,
Believing that Santa his duty would keep!

In the still of the night, I did hear Santa call,
To Rudolph, to Dasher, to Dancer to all,
"Let's haste on our journey," was what he did say,
"We have toys to deliver, before Christmas Day."

I watched as with alacrity he stepped out of his sleigh,
"I'll be back in a jiffy," to his Reindeer did say,
With a sack full of toys down the chimney did go,
In a jiffy he was back, with a soft ho, ho, ho!

As he returned to his sleigh with, "My beauties lets go,
No time must be wasted for as you all know,
The world's children are excited about Christmas Day,
So come then my beauties up, up and away."

I watched as he gave a slight tug on the reins.
With that they took flight and were airborne again,
As they circled our town, I heard Santa say,
"Thank you, my Reindeer, for pulling my sleigh."

"To Dasher, to Dancer to Prancer and Vixen,
To Comet, to Cupid, to Donner and Blitzen,
And also, to Rudolph our vanguard in flight,
My nine faithful helpers on Christmas Eve Night."

Before he flew off to faraway places,
With toys for all children of different races,
He flew down where I was at the town's Christmas tree,
And smiled as he threw a present to me.

"Well caught my man," he said with a chuckle,
As he loosened his belt a good space at the buckle,
"I've been eating too much; can't you tell by my tummy?
Those treats the children leave taste, yummy, yummy, yummy!"

I thanked him for coming year after year,
"It's a pleasure," said he, "for me to come here.
What would I do with all of my toys?
If I didn't give them to all the good girls and boys."

As he looked at his watch he said, "Gosh, I must leave,
But I'll be back here again next Christmas Eve,
As for me I must travel, I must play my part,
To bring laughter and joy to every child's heart."

DG Tandra

*May your Christmas be happy from my heart this I say,
I hope tomorrow will be, your best Christmas day!*

Belfast is Buzzing again!

For too long we feared to enter,
The City that we call our own,
Lest exploding bombs and flying bullets,
Would escort us prematurely, to our eternal home.

For long our capital City, Belfast,
Had to hang her head in shame,
For the years of warring conflict,
Brought much misery and pain.

She was blasted, wounded, cheated,
Her heart was broken time after time,
Pounded by salvoes of hatred,
Yet herself guiltless of any crime!

The buzz she had, had been anaesthetised,
By the troubles and the strife,
The wail of the warning siren,
Caused a running for dear life!

The troubles have now all ended,
Thankfully, they are part of our past,
The future looks bright for our City,
As we work the peace process to last.

Like the Phoenix she has risen from the ashes,
Refused to give up the ghost,
With new vigour, ambition, excitement,
She now is the most perfect host!

There's a buzz in the air, I can hear it,
It's a soft, soothing sweet melody,
Uplifts the spirit and causes a song,
Perfect for our sanity.

The buzz in the air, I can feel it,
Its vibes reach into my soul,
Causes my feet a tap tapping,
Fulfilling a part of its role.

That buzz in the air let me tell it,
I want you to share in it too,
Wherever you're from I want you to know,
There's a special buzz buzzing for you!

So come to where the buzz is buzzing,
Be part of the craic, laughter, and song,
See the sights of our beautiful City,
Join with the happy-go-lucky throng.

Be part of the buzz that is buzzing,
Shout out with might and with main,
With a thunderous roar let the whole world know,
That Belfast is buzzing again!

A Dream for Peace!

I had a dream not in sleep but in reality,
The perfect panacea for every ill there'd be,
If the peoples of this world would dream along with me,
This world would be a better place for all humanity!

No need for bombs and bullets or threatening oratory,
No stockpiles of destructive weapons, beasts of predatory,
No display of military might terrorising vulnerable society,
Such belligerent behaviour we don't need, peace is our priority.

I had a dream the fruit of which would produce Utopia,
No more fears, no more tears no more phobia,
No tyrants, no dictators, no greedy grabbing louts,
No stalking and no muggings, in safety walk about.

The dream I had will be good for all, no injury will it cause,
But hope, health and happiness when adheres to my dream laws,
The bullying by the superpowers will be a thing of the past,
When they forget about their ego, and work for a peace to last!

No more war declarations when diplomacy reigns supreme,
Peace gains the upper hand when held in highest esteem,
It will not war with anyone nor cause hurtful tears to fall,
The world needs peace, so let us all hasten to its call!

There is nothing glorious or romantic on the battlefields of blood,
Banish thoughts of glory as through death and muck you trudge,
Such of carnage let it be the happenings of the past,
And work indefatigably for peace that must be our task!

Peace it is a blessing wherever it is found,
No curse it carries with it but with hope it does abound,
It will not cheat nor rob you, but reward you with its smile,
For it carries in its bosom what makes living well worthwhile!

Erin's best

The sunshine of our great Father's love,
Has shone upon you from above,
The Lord who made the sky and sea,
Has caused my Rose to bloom for me!

O Irish Rose my own Irish Rose,
There's not another flower that grows,
In any part of Ireland fair,
That I would want my life to share.

Today we stood in God's own sight,
And vowed our love for the rest of life,
And whatever that our life will be,
I will be with you; you will be with me.

When I am old and life's almost through,
Twill reminisce sweet thoughts of you,
I will tell you then, as I tell you now,
My Irish Rose is still my pride and joy!

O Irish Rose sweet Irish Rose,
To me the fairest flower that grows,
Today you look lovely in full bloom,
You have made me proud to be the groom.

My life today tastes oh so sweet,
For I got the girl who made it complete,
You are that special flower that grows,
Erin's best, my own Irish Rose!

Peace at Last!

The Pessimist his message spread of darkness, doom, and gloom,
The picture that he painted sadly left no room
For better days and fresh new ways when, Ireland would be free,
From years of warring conflict to peace and tranquillity!

The bombs, the guns, the killings, the hatred, and the strife
Is what you've gotten used too; they are now part of life.
So don't look for solutions, as there are no magic pills,
That will bring about Utopia and cure you of your ills!

The Optimist his message was like music to the heart,
He had no distressing statements that he wanted to impart,
His words the antithesis of what Pessimistic had to say,
For he could see the clouds of strife and trouble roll away!

His words were so uplifting when you heard what he did say,
The bombings and the burnings, they have had their day.
The hatred and the bitterness, to peace they shall give way,

Then there'll be a future bright when wrong causes go away!

The Realist to the Podium stepped up with this to say,
I agree with Optimist, we can see a better day,
The killing guns are silent; the bomb blast is no more,
But we need not be complacent; there is still much work in store!

The work is just beginning, and the journey will be long,
There are obstacles to overcome as you try to right the wrong.
There are many uncertainties and hindrances in the way,
With courage and commitment, Peace shall win the day!

The struggle you must not give up, even though the cost is high,
Prepare yourself for criticism, slander, and the lie.
Don't be deflected from the task, you know that you must do,
Resolve it deep within your heart to see this process through.

You owe it to yourselves my friends and to your fellowman,
To build a better future and promote this our homeland.
This message you must spread abroad, it's part of your vital task,
To tell the world, in Ireland there is Peace at Last!

DG Tandra

Peace at last, peace at last,
Thank God we have peace at last!

Poems of my Homeland

* Saint Patrick

www.ingramcontent.com/pod-product-compliance
Lightning Source LLC
LaVergne TN
LVHW051219070526
838200LV00064B/4973